The quarterly journal of *21st Century Chinese Poetry* was founded with the intention of introducing modern Chinese poetry to readers worldwide.

Modern Chinese poetry was born from the broader intellectual movement that took place in China in the early part of the 20th century, known as the May-Fourth Movement (1917-1921); for the first time in history, vernacular Chinese was accepted as a legitimate poetic voice. Since then, nearly a century has passed by and this poetic experiment hasn't stopped evolving but only accelerated recently because of the easy exchange of styles and ideas over cyberspace. This is an eye-opening, exciting and even confounding experience for both the poets and the readers.

The editor-and-translator team of *21st Century Chinese Poetry* selects some of the best poems written in Chinese by today's poets from all geographical areas.

Pathsharers LLC
560 N St SW, N-812, Washington DC 20024
Copyright @ 2013 by Pathsharers LLC

All poems are translated by permissions of authors
All applications for any use of any poems or quotations
from them should be made to
Pathsharers LLC
560 N St SW, N-812, Washington DC 20024
editor@modernchinesepoetry.com

ISBN 978-1-939426-05-5
ISSN 2166-3688 (Print--Bilingual)
ISSN 2164-1870 (Online)

21st Century Chinese Poetry

No. 8

廿一世纪中国诗歌，第八辑

Edited and Translated
by
Meifu Wang, Michael Soper, Steven Townsend

A Pathsharers Book

CONTENTS:

女儿红 Blushing Red 8
    陈敏 | Chen Min

哎哟，妈妈 Ow, Mama! 12
    宋雨 | Song Yu

挽歌 Elegy 14
    宋雨 | Song Yu

河 River 16
    宋雨 | Song Yu

春到台儿庄 Spring Comes to Tai'erzhuang 18
    李云（七月的海） | Li Yun

在石祖林 At Shizu Stone Ruin 22
    李云（七月的海） | Li Yun

夜晚 At Night 24
    翟文熙 | Zhai Wenxi

一天 A Day 26
    翟文熙 | Zhai Wenxi

遗物 Items in My Estate 28
    翟文熙 | Zhai Wenxi

在圣玛丽娅医院 In Saint Maria's Hospital 30
    姚風 | Yao Feng

大海真的不需要这些东西
Ocean Really Doesn't Need These Things 32
 姚風 | Yao Feng

植物人 Vegetative Man 34
 姚風 | Yao Feng

情人 Beloved 36
 姚風 | Yao Feng

云南的黄昏 An Afternoon in Yunnan 38
 娜夜 | Na Ye

标准 The Standards 40
 娜夜 | Na Ye

拉不楞寺短歌 Song of Labrang Monastery 42
 娜夜 | Na Ye

那一天是哪一天 hen Was That? 44
 娜夜 | Na Ye

濯影寒泉 Tree Shadow in Cold Spring 46
 巫丁 | Wuding

莲叶乱叫 The Lotus Pond Jam Session 48
 巫丁 | Wuding

三杯两盏 Three Cups and Two Shots 50
 巫丁 | Wuding

一些事物被重新安排 Things Get Rearranged 52

    黄礼孩 | Huang Lihai

小 兽 A Little Critter 54

    黄礼孩 | Huang Lihai

背影 Silhouette 56

    黄礼孩 | Huang Lihai

夸父 Kua Fu 58

    宋惠元（柳思）| Song Huiyuan

雪的预告总是不准的
Predictions of Snow Are Rarely Accurate 60

    宋惠元（柳思）| Song Huiyuan

山岩 Mountain Crag 62

    王美富 | Meifu Wang

战俘 Prisoners of War 64

    王美富 | Meifu Wang

致梅尔维尔 To Melville 68

    王美富 | Meifu Wang

Information about Contributors 70

女儿红

文 / 陈敏

女儿红，女儿红……

比包谷酒比老婆红火的名字，
燃烧得割漆的汉子们眼睛发直。
是该红火的时候，便做次新娘子。

在秋风唢呐的护送下，
羞羞答答姗姗走过徒崖。
徒崖坎子挡不住，
纷飞的岁月挡不住。

漂亮得红艳欲滴，
流光溢彩得出奇。
（哪个割漆的汉子不想你哟）
直到少男们吆喝，老头们吆喝，
敞开怀奶孩子香喷喷热烘烘的少妇 和
眨巴着眼皮小脚婆婆一齐吆喝：

女儿红，女儿红、
——啊，那漫山遍野的女儿红！

Blushing Red
 ----Subtitle: The Lacquer Tree
    by Chen Min

Blushing Red, maiden in red...

More than the corn liquor, more than their wives' names,
she inflames the lacquer-tree men, eyes staring wide.
What a propitious time to become someone's bride.

Following the autumn wind, as the horns blow and blow,
shyly and slowly across the precipice, there she goes.
Uplands between the fields, no use trying to stop her.
The gap in years and months, no use trying to stop her.

Sweet and beautiful, provoking the deepest desires,
Time spills its colors on her, producing fire.
Oh, which lacquer-tree cutter would not want you?
Until young men call, and elders urge them on,
and nursing mothers with sweet warm bosoms join in,
and dry-eyed foot-binding grandmothers chime in:

Blushing Red, maiden in red,
around the bend and over the hills,
Oh, Blushing Red, Yo!

这些一长排布扣子拦不住欲望的汉子们，
酸咸菜红薯糊糊的思想者和叛逆者们，
一边嘟囔着女儿红的风流韵事，
一边喘着气把眼睛瞪得比酒盅大比酒盅有神，
眺望着
这个比阴历年醇美比山坡久长的时辰。

——女儿红，女儿红，
那漫天遍野的女儿红哟！

These long rows of buttons don't hold back a man's desire,
the pickle-munching, potato-eating thinkers and
    revolutionaries
mumbling the affairs of Blushing Red, half gasping and
    panting,
staring eyeballs as big as wine cups, as spirited as wine cups,
gazing at a hill of blushing red, redder than New Year, dated
    earlier than the hills.

Blushing Red, maiden in red,
coloring heaven and all below,
Oh, Blushing Red, Yo!

哎哟，妈妈
　　文/宋雨

哎哟，妈妈
妈妈，我真的不喜欢你再给我梳头
我坐不住。外面的小草都发芽了，妈妈
你还要给我扎上红头绳，绿头绳
一边骂我是黄毛丫头，一边拧着麻花。
伙伴们在野外喊杀阵阵，穆桂英就要挂帅了
我的杨宗保他，他，他
他在等待一个失而复得的我
哎哟，妈妈。
桃木梳子不小心生出了桃红
我这个命犯桃花的
无可救药的
你的野丫头

Ow, Mama!
    by Song Yu

Ow, Mama!
I really don't like you combing my hair so much.
I can't sit still. Outside, grasses are all sprouting, Mama.
You still want to give me red hair ties and green hair ties.
While calling me a little spoiled brat,
you braided my hair like twisted dough.
My comrades in the field are shouting battle cries;
Mu Guiying is about to lead the charge.
My man Yang Zhongbao, him, him, him,
he waits for me to return like a hero missing in action.
Ow, Mama!
A peach wood comb is giving me a peach red stain.
I am doomed to offend with my wild roaming heart.
You cannot cure
your little spoiled brat.

挽歌

　　文 /宋雨

是一个乳白色的早晨
从一场美梦中苏醒
梦中，渴望过的奇迹
仿佛一切热爱的离去的事物回转身
又一次来到了身边
我看到地平线
在前方缓慢升起
那是如何来临的光芒呢
此刻正把它银灰色柔软的叶子抖落
并且洒向来路或深深的去路
叫她圣母，叫她女神
圣者的妻子
我的母亲……
我该叫她缪斯的使者吗？
她居然叫我：孩子
望着我
世人望着婴儿的眼神那样望着我
她给了我圣水
答应我留在这世上的一切罪过
都将得到应有的忏悔
她带来了我最需要的东西
一个精美的针线盒
它将缝整齐我褴褛的见不得人的伤口
她将带着我体面地回家。

Elegy
    by Song Yu

It is a milk-white morning;
I awaken from a beautiful dream.
In the dream, the miracle I yearned for
seemed to have returned
with everything I once loved but lost.
I watched a peaceful horizon
slowly ascending before me.
How can there be such radiance there?
Then, lithe, silver-gray leaves trembled and fell,
spilling along a path leading to the future
and connected with the mysterious past.
Call her holy mother, call her a goddess,
wife of the holiest,
my mother . . .
Should I call her messenger for Muse?
To my surprise, she calls me: Child,
and examines me
the way people examine babies.
She gave me holy water,
and promised me a chance to repent
for all of my misdeeds.
She brought me the most essential thing,
an exquisite needle case.
It will neatly sew and hide my ragged mortal wounds.
She will watch me return home with dignity.

河

文 / 宋雨

没有比克兰河更熟悉我的河了
出生的时候,我在它的东边
成长的时候,我在它的西边
出嫁的时候,我又在它的东边
爱一个人的时候,他在西边
恨一个人的时候,他在东边

River
    by Song Yu

No one knows me better than the Kelan River.
When I was born, I landed on its east side.
Growing up, I lived on its west side.
When I married, I again lived on its east side.
Then I loved a man, he lived on the west side.
When I detested someone, he lived on the east side.

春到台儿庄

　　文/李云（七月的海）

台儿庄台儿庄，昨天你看见战争
今晨你看见了春天
你看万家大院的海棠开了，白里透粉
冷艳馨香的一大片

冷艳馨香的一大片啊
这一定与我有关
昨夜我架着星空而来
今早，我却被一树海棠花留下

台儿庄台儿庄，此刻
我与你站在一起，为无限春光修辞
战争，和平
和平，战争
已让我先后判若两人

台儿庄，当花朵在你怀中
跳舞的一刻
我必须带着记忆的忧伤
凝固在这里
凝固在记忆里

Spring Comes to Tai'erzhuang
    by Li Yun

Tai'erzhuang, Tai'erzhuang, yesterday you saw war,
this morning you saw spring.
You see, the crabapple trees in Mr. Wan's courtyards
are now blooming, white inside, a touch of pink,
a serene field of sweet scent and charm.

Sweet scent and charm, no end of it, Ah!
I am not at all detached from this.
Last night I came by to deliver the stars for you.
This morning I stayed because of a flowering tree.

Tai'erzhuang, Tai'erzhuang, right now,
here with you, I sing the splendor of spring.
War, Peace,
Peace, War,
they have made me a different person.

Tai'er Village, while these blossoms
dance with and around you.
I must bear an old sorrow,
congealed inside here,
congealed within the memory.

噢,台儿庄,我不是花妖
我曾是你这片土地上流血的女战士
在转动的晨光里
发出诵经的微响
唵嘛呢叭咪吽
我终将要被通灵的僧人带走

Oh, Tai'erzhuang, I am not a flower witch,
but a woman warrior, born here, now bleeding for you.
I hear a low chant in the revolving light,
Om-mani-pad-me-hum.
A little monk will be coming to summon me.

在石祖林

文 / 李云(七月的海)

如此恍惚,仿佛在很久以前来过
风是凉的,月光也凉

石头也是凉的吗
哦,这圣物
当然,有时也是蠢物

"唉,真不懂姐姐把这冰凉的造物
置于人间
是何用意?"

几世轮回,我已经问过神仙姐姐多次
今夜,都懒得问了

有人说到图腾,有人说到父系氏族。
那些醉翁之意。

当然,我也想到父亲
想起我的儿子,在石祖林

在石祖林,我抬头看见了天上的月亮
哦,月亮爬上来
月亮又落下去

在石祖林,我独爱那纯净的
纯净的月光

At Shizu Stone Ruin
    by Li Yun

It is almost like a daze, déjà vu,
to feel this cool wind, this cold moonlight.

Are stones cold too?
Oh, this one is a monster,
but, of course, it could have been a hoax.

"Um, can't figure out why Thou placed them here.
Why on earth?
What's the point?"

For each of its reincarnations, I asked my goddess sister the
    same question,
but tonight I won't go through it again.

Some say these stones are totems, or pillars of patriarchy.
Ah, people can be nostalgic!

But of course, I am thinking of my father,
and my son too, here at this stone ruin.

At the Shizu Stone Ruin, the moon is high.
Oh, yes, she comes up
and goes down.

Next to these stone totems, all that I love
is the untainted moonlight.

夜晚

　　文 /翟文熙

他闲置的鼻子成为一个老式绅士
的烟斗。时间是一个假象，
包括吊钟指向的位置，头脑浮现的
以时间为轴的图像。
"没有人愿意这个时候入睡，除非他是柚子脑袋。
他这样想着，秋风踩着台阶爬上了
弹簧一样的树枝。
月亮吊诡地挂在塔尖。
女人在房间里睡觉。
椅子与椅子自由地交谈。
无形的思想像物品由主人保管。
他们不轻易交换。
"一杯啤酒的泡沫足以将灵魂溺死。"
但是他仍旧清醒。
不远处，孤单的夜莺把漆黑的山顶
当做试音室。
他的身体倒伏在卧榻上，正被
窗外涌进来的月光
慢慢地搬动。

At Night
by Zhai Wenxi

His nose has fallen into disuse like a gentleman's pipe.
But we see only superficial time,
the framework instilled by a pendulum clock.
" No one wants to doze off now unless he is a peabrain."
Just as he reminds himself, a breeze climbs up the stairs
to ride on the springy tree branches.
The moon clings to a spire like playing an old slapstick.
A woman sleeps in the room.
Chairs gossip with each other.
People guard their thoughts,
which they seldom exchange.
"Beer froth can drown a soul."
but he stays sober.
Not too far away, a lonely nightingale tests his voice
on the dark mountaintop.
He lies on his belly,
and slowly moves across the room,
floating on the moonlight
that has come through the window and flooded the room.

一天

文 / 翟文熙

我把黑夜和白天颠倒着使用。
我终日开着灯,坏掉的灯泡,
让它继续坏着。
一天喝完一包普洱,洗衣机反复
涮洗衣服,只是因为懒得
晾到阳台上。
写下满纸的汉代木牍文字,丢弃在
地板上。再也没有
我喜欢的事物了。除了沉默和冥想,
现在我想造一只鸟,一棵树,
但我不希望
它们跟我说话,或者拆掉时钟,
倾听心脏
在秒针上跳动。
困倦后我会在灯光中睡去。
之后的时间,几乎可以
把一切忘记。

A Day
    by Zhai Wenxi

I do not treat Day and Night with common sense.
The lights stay on all the time, and the burnt-out bulbs
    remain.
Although Puer tea is always kept fresh,
the washer can wash the old clothes again and again
because I don't feel like hanging them up.
I've been practicing tomb script from the Han Dynasty,
the paper is now discarded on the floor.
Nothing seems fanciful any more.
Other than silence and meditation,
I would like to make a bird and a tree,
but not for them to talk with me.
I also would like to take apart the clock
and count my heartbeats with the seconds hand.
Doze off with the light on when tired.
What comes next is for time to erase most memories.

遗物

　　文 /翟文熙

我拥有的天赋、骨头。
我说过的方言，看过的河流和岛屿，鸟群和星宿
我在厩中喂过的牛羊。
甚至我染上的每一场疾病。
都像是一件遗物。月亮静静地
反射着日光，风吹着
古老庙宇的廊柱，不是廊柱而是我们的灵魂发出颤音。
青苔在石壁上生长——
衰败的气息连接着掌心的暗纹。
我们活着不是活着，只是为了
跟树交换氧气。
我赋予我全部的意义：生长、死亡、交换
沉默地对抗。

Items in My Estate
   by Zhai Wenxi

My genius and my bones,
the dialects I know,
the rivers, islands, island chains and galaxies I saw,
the cattle and sheep I fed in the barn,
the illnesses I contracted,
all of them are items I left to my estate.
I see the silent moon reflecting the sun,
hear the pillars of old temples echo the cries of my soul
when the wind is blowing,
and read the lichens on the stonewall the way
I read my palms for clues of life and death.
Therefore I know
to live is not merely an act of persistence
but to commune with trees through transpiration.
My estate includes everything that gives meaning to my life:
growth, death, exchange, and silent resistance.

在圣玛丽娅医院
　　文/姚風

从白色的被单中,你向我伸出一只手
它修长,枯干,涂着蔻丹的指甲
像梅花,把冬天的树枝照耀
这些指甲,这些花,你一次次剪掉
又让它们一次次怒放

它们,位于你生活和身体的边缘
但总是这么洁净,这么鲜艳
哪怕在这所
和国家一样混乱的国家医院

抓住你的手,感到褐色的血管隆起
血液蠕动,从红色的指尖折返
记得你在书中说,在死亡的肉体中
指甲是最后腐烂的物质

In Saint Maria's Hospital
by Yao Feng

From under the white bed sheet
you turn to me and extend a hand,
slender, withered,
red cardamom on your fingernails
like plum blossoms lightening up winter twigs.
These fingernails, these blossoms,
you once and again clip away,
once and again allow them to bloom.

They are the outermost bits of your body,
yet always so clean, so fresh-colored,
even in this place
with all the chaos of a public hospital,
situated in a chaotic country.

I take your hand and feel the ripples
of blood through brown-colored veins,
pulsing back and forth through your red finger tips.
Remember, in your book you said:
We live in dying bodies,
and fingernails are the last to decompose.

大海真的不需要这些东西

　　文 /姚风

在德里加海滩,大海
不停地翻滚
像在拒绝,像要把什么还给我们
我们看见光滑的沙滩上
丢弃的酒瓶子、针筒、卫生纸、避孕套

我们嘿嘿一笑,我们的快乐和悲伤
越来越依赖身体,越来越需要排泄
光滑的沙滩上,有我们丢弃的
酒瓶子、针筒、卫生纸、避孕套

但大海真的不需要这些东西
甚至不需要
如此高级的人类

Ocean Really Doesn't Need These Things
    by Yao Feng

On Derita Beach, in the sea and the sand,
the ocean rolls and tumbles
as if it wants to return something to us.
We see unwanted wine bottles on the glossy beach,
and syringes, tissues, condoms.

We giggle, the more our happiness and sadness
depend on physical activities, the more we need to flush
onto the glossy beach our unwanted wine bottles,
syringes, tissues, and condoms.

But the ocean really doesn't need these things,
not even the high points of our humanity.

植物人

　　文 /姚風

人从地上站立起来
就开始用语言命名大千世界
玫瑰花开花落
不知道自己叫做玫瑰
君子兰也不知道
自己和君子有何关系
此时我远离语言学和植物学
无言地坐在老张的床边
他浑身插满管子
像一株茂盛的植物
我转移视线，窗外的树
已经伸展所有的叶子
在玻璃上投下快乐的斑影
我最后看了一眼老张
他睁开了双眼
但他什么也没有看见

Vegetative Man
    by Yao Feng

One day Man began to walk erect, and didn't wait
to assign names to everything under the sun.
But from bloom to fade,
a rose has no idea she's called Rose,
nor does a Gentleman Orchid know
what he's got to do with any gentleman.
But right now, linguistics and taxonomy are irrelevant
when I sit with my old buddy Zhang on his bedside.
He has tubes up and down his body
like a luxuriant plant.
I move my line of vision
and notice the trees outside the window
are proliferous with leaves,
casting cheerful specks on the glass.
I look at my old buddy Zhang one last time,
there he opens both eyes
but not a thing does he see.

情人

　　文/姚风

在骨灰盒里
我的每一粒骨灰还保存着炉膛的余热
鲜花簇拥,对人世我恋恋不舍
我听见哀乐沉重徐缓
亲人节制但悲痛地抽泣
来宾在鞠躬时骨骼和衣服发出细微的声响
大公无私,光明磊落,低音的悼词
删除了我一生中的瑕疵
在悼词的停顿之间,我更听见了
站在最后一排右数第三个女人的低哭
突然间,骨灰盒闪出火光
那是我化悲痛为力量
每一粒骨灰又燃烧了一回

Beloved
    by Yao Feng

Inside the urn, every speck of my ashes
is still hot from the heat of the furnace.
Surrounded by fresh flowers, how reluctant I am to leave this
    world.
I hear the dirge, heavy and slow.
Relatives restrain themselves, but can't hold back sobs.
Guests are bowing, bones and clothing rustling.
"Just and fair, honorable and upright."
The somber eulogy omits all the mistakes I made.
Between the pauses I hear
a woman weep, third from the right, last row.
Suddenly, flames burst out from the urn.
That is me
turning grief into strength,
that is my ashes,
every speck on fire again.

云南的黄昏

　　文 /娜夜

云南的黄昏

我们并没谈起诗歌

夜晚也没交换所谓的苦难

两个女人

都不是母亲

我们谈论星空和康德

特蕾莎修女和心脏内科

谈论无神论者迷信的晚年

一些事物的美在于它的阴影

另一个角度：没有孩子使我们得以完整

An Afternoon in Yunnan
    by Na Ye

Afternoon in Yunnan,
no mention of poetry,
no exchanges about human suffering before sleep,
we are two women,
neither is a mother.
We talk about the starry sky and Kant,
Mother Teresa and Cardiology.
We muse about those atheists that turned pious in old age,
and assert shadows can be prettier than the objects.
There is another perspective: being childless keeps us whole.

标准

　　文 /娜夜

我手里只有一票
眼前却晃着两个美人
最后一轮了
评委席上
我的耐心和审美疲劳都到了极限
我等她们
换上泳装
或薄纱
再次晃到我眼前
果然
更充分的裸露
使她们的美有了区别
我的一票果断而坚定
不是她的三围比例
是她的身体摆动众人目光时
一种追求毁灭的　气质

The Standards
    by Na Ye

There is only one vote left
but two beauty-pageant finalists.
This is the last round.
In the judges corner,
my patience and aesthetic taste are worn out,
therefore I waited eagerly for them
to change into swimming suits
or see-through gowns
and float towards me just one more time.
Indeed this is happening.
With more bare flesh,
the secrets of their beauty is now discernible.
My vote is absolute and decisive,
not based on BWH proportion,
but by the way her body sways and lures our eyes;
she has an air,
the air of a martyr.

拉不楞寺短歌
　　文/娜夜

我的围巾被风吹进寺院的时候
那个与我擦间而过　呼呼冒着热气的喇嘛
呼呼地　下山干什么呢？

街上的藏人少了　集市散了
格桑花顺着大夏河的流水走远了

相面人把手伸进我钱包的时候
那个瞎眼打坐的老阿妈是用什么看见的呢？

接着　她又看见
天堂寺以西
她的小卓玛已经上学了
牧区的春风温暖
教室明亮
鹰　在黑板上飞得很高

今生啊——
来世——
风在风中轮回

凡事宽容　凡事相信　凡事忍耐
--我以为这对我眼下的生活有用
但我并没快乐起来

——我没说啊　佛是怎么知道的呢？

Song of Labrang Monastery
    by Na Ye

A wind came by and blew my scarf to the monastery,
it was then when we passed each other, rubbing shoulders.
Ah, Lama, you were huffing and puffing, going down the
    mountain. But why?

The bazaar never opens now because fewer and fewer
    Tibetans come to the street.
The River Daxia has carried so many Kelsang Metogs with it
    to the sea.

A blind old granny, in meditation, saw it when the
    fortuneteller reached for my purse.
How did she see?

She also sees,
beyond the Temple of Heaven,
the spring wind reaching the grassland,
and her little Zhuoma going to school.
The classroom is bright,
and a hawk soars over the blackboard.

Ah, right here and right now--
Or the next life--
The wind is always changing.

"Bear all things, believe all things, hope all things, endure all
    things."
--I thought life would be better if I followed this teaching.
But it did not cheer me up.

--Oh, I didn't say a word about it. How does Buddha know
    my heart?

那一天是哪一天

　　文/娜夜

敲开门 你在喝水
你腾开一个合适的位置 给我
不明不暗
有着来去和伸缩的自由
零星的落雪
像我们零星的话语
你在喝水
我看你喝水
你的梦幻触手可及

——那一天是哪一天

"太深了"我对自己说
你的手触到了我的伤口
"不是这 是这"
我拿着你的手
放在了心的位置

When Was That?
   by Na Ye

When I knocked at your door,
you were drinking a glass of water.
You made room for me
and put me at ease.
The lighting was just right.
Snowflakes came down gently
at the same pace as our conversation.
You were drinking water,
and I was watching you.
Your dream was within reach.

That was when?

"It cut too deep", I told myself.
Your hand touched my wound.
"Not here, it's here."
I held your hand
and laid it on my heart.

濯影寒泉

　　文/巫丁

冬水刺骨,树和树的影子
等待一去不回的暖风
三月的花朵住得遥远,让它
呼吸散乱一池,而水波不兴

等了千年,现在的气侯
没有定式,没有人在意树
在水湄举丫丫叉叉的纠结
如何想要抓牢时间的手

自己离自己都那么远
枝条挂不住往事的叶片
绿意盎然只是过去的荣耀
从这个空间到另一个空间

日复一日,三月再没有打马来过
只得在水中拼命洗自己的影子
季节外面,时光外边
这棵树还没有学会伤感

Tree Shadow in Cold Spring
   by Wuding

Wintry days, the cold spring sends a chill to the bones.
A tree and his shadow wait for the return of spring zephyr.
But the flowers of March are remote, and his impatience
      reverberates
across the pond, though the cold spring is untouched.

A thousand years of waiting,
the weather has veered into anomalies.
All the while no one ever noticed that the tree's scraggly
      limbs
were arching over the water as if trying to grasp the passing
      moments.

He is alienated from himself,
losing leaves, each with an imprint
of the splendors of the past,
drifting from one place to another.

Day in and day out, there is still no sign of March,
the tree does all he can to freshen up his shadow in the cold
      spring.
He has no idea of what melancholy is
beyond the change of season and the change of time.

莲叶乱叫

　　文/巫丁

水滴纷纷逃离天空 一场豪雨
让布衣的颜色 淡了又深
铺天盖地的鸣蝉唱红歌
继续 季节喧嚣的传统
而风在吹 风自由自在

晨光中的一支莲蓬
摇摆 一池莲叶乱乱地轻叫
昨夜萤虫熄灯 蛙声参差不齐
雨 浇湿所有的稻花
不着调 蛙们不唱丰年

这时候怀旧 迷人而危险
风起 吹动那些光线
吹不动日子 日子坚硬如铁
碰痛旧时光中的莽撞少年……

The Lotus Pond Jam Session
    by Wuding

Quickly they flee the sky
and come down as heavy rain,
falling on me and darkening my sun-bleached jersey.
A brood of cicadas sing a red-army song,
energizing the air of this summer carnival.
The wind blows on, minding its own business.

A lotus seedpod sways in the twilight
above a pond of leaves, all gently caroling.
The fireflies didn't light up the night before,
leaving the toads to croak in and out.
The rain kept falling, striking the rice flowers.
But the toads sang out of tune, nowhere near a harvest song.

It's tempting but too dangerous to look back.
The wind is picking up, bending the sunlight,
but it cannot move an old iron bloc of days
that rubbed against the skin of my tempestuous youth.

三杯两盏

　　文/巫丁

一饮 再饮
三杯两盏之后

秋天向南
气候找不着北
月到天心
磁场也玩漂移

风就凉了起来
暑气无踪

摸不着脉门
只摸住草里的秋虫
欲言又止的虫鸣
乘着一阵清风

深夜 一饮 再饮
莲籽茶 淡如月

Three Cups and Two Shots
    by Wuding

Drink, don't stop.
With three cups and two shots in the belly,

autumn seems to migrate south
as it has lost its way north.
The moon moves to center stage,
forcing the magnetic field to realign.

Feel this wind and chill out,
for summer is gone.

My pulses are calm and slow, but I can feel
the autumn cricket rustling in the grass
unsure whether to speak or not to speak,
but soon it is gone with the wind.

It's past midnight, but drink, drink another cup of
this lotus tea, a taste of the unearthly moon.

一些事物被重新安排
　　文/黄礼孩

世界潜藏在细微的变化里
早上咖啡飘出香味,如从巢房里射出霞光
窗外低矮的橄榄树,还保持着凌晨以来的潮气
细碎的脚步声把听觉带到远处
而出海归来的渔人,他坐在院子里
看一只在树上寻找食物的小鸟。他写信回国
在自己的梦里。海洋遗忘,冰山坍塌
就在此时,神所珍爱的事物,被重新安排

Things Get Rearranged
    by Huang Lihai

The world's secrets hide in slight variations.
The coffee aroma in the morning air feels like the glow from
        a honeycomb,
while, outside the window, the olive grove still soaks in the
        twilight mist.
Tiny footsteps follow little sounds to distant places,
but the fisherman has returned, and is sitting in the courtyard
watching a bird foraging in the trees. He still dreams of
sending letters home. The sea forgets and the glacier calves
        icebergs,
that's how all the charitable things under the sun
get rearranged.

小 兽

　　文 /黄礼孩

一只小兽从草丛穿过
我与它隔着 一米月光的距离
草色晃动
淹没了夜晚的尾巴

像传说中的女神
把梦铺开
柔软地晾在大地上

一个干净的人
福音要降临到她的身上
我低下头来
凝视裸露的脚
大地已安息

我依然感受到你身体内
流动的月光

A Little Critter
    by Huang Lihai

Three feet of moonlight away,
a little critter zigzags through the grass,
the green waves
soon drown its tail.

They say it was a goddess
that rolled out a soft field on earth--
soft because it's a mat of dreams.

She purified herself
to receive benevolence from above.
And when I look down,
I see my bare feet
and peace on earth.

I also see how moonlight
slowly moves across your body.

背影

　　文 /黄礼孩

背影与生活有什么关系
有人说出它隐藏的杀机

背对我们而去的人
掐断了明天就要到来的诚意
生活怎值得信赖
我转身离去消失于人群

这个时代没有伟人诞生
你望见的是谁的背影……

Silhouette
    by Huang Lihai

How is a silhouette related to life?
Someone pointed out its hidden power to kill.

People who walked away from us
choked off our exuberance for the next day.
How can we continue to trust life after that?
This question made me turn away from the crowd.

Where is our great modern-day figure?
Whose silhouette did you see earlier?

夸父

　　　文 /宋惠元 （柳思）

当光明离我远去黑幕乘虚而入的时候
我知道太阳去了哪里
太阳也走不远的，它最多是踩着荆棘的山路踽踽独行
像个犯错的孩子
躲到山后去了，或者像个坠落的椰球
被海上的波浪冲到对岸去了
所以我必须去追逐
我不为人类，我只为一场游戏
为我自己，我去追回太阳
我知道我起步迟了脚步慢了
但我看见了太阳滚落的方向
只要我坚持
只要再坚持12小时
只要熬过这并不漫长的长夜
我一定会再次追上光明的时刻。谁跟着我，谁就能重见光明
因为，太阳是我脚下的一个皮球

Kua Fu
    by Song Huiyuan

Just as the light departs farther and farther and darkness rolls
    in to fill the void,
I know where the sun goes.
Sunlight cannot go too far, at most it is trampling the
    brambles of the hills, walking in solitude,
like a delinquent child hiding behind a hill,
or a fallen coconut tossed by the sea to reach the other shore.
And so, I must pursue it,
not for mankind, but for my own amusement.
For myself, I chase the sun.
I know I started late and walked slowly,
but I saw the direction it was rolling down.
If only I can persevere,
if only I can persist for another twelve little hours,
if only I can endure through this finite stretch of night,
surely I will catch up with the light again.
Whoever follows me, they can again see the light,
because, the sun is my football.

雪的预告总是不准的
　　　文 /宋惠元 （柳思）

妻子说了
雪的预告总是不准的

好比我的归期
女儿都盼着

说好昨日来
今天还没有到

来了也呆不住几天
就化开了，就不见了

有时还真不如不来
妻子说了

除了把家门弄弄湿
把条条归路弄弄湿

雪有什么好
雪有什么好？还那么冷净

Predictions of Snow Are Rarely Accurate
    by Song Huiyuan

My wife said,
"Predictions of snow are rarely accurate."

Just like on the day of my scheduled return,
my daughters are all waiting.

It was agreed that it would be yesterday,
but still no sign of it today.

Even if it does show up, in just a few days
all is melted, vanished.

May as well be a no show,
my wife said.

Besides leaving the front door wet,
besides leaving every home-coming road wet,

what good is snow?
What good is snow? And it's so cold!

山岩

文 / 王美富

我寄居于旅途，
散漫的臆想像小书僮悄悄跟上。
无须抬头，已见低垂的天幕。

他，来得比夜更突兀；
他，屹立于深海之中；
他，用巨爪扣住地球。

在冰冷的海里，在墨绿的海里，
他肩骨嶙峋，背负坎坷的命运，
与地球一起旋转；是他在挡驾风雨。

臆想悄悄地来，悄悄地去，
我的日子也同样飘忽。
天睡在海的胸脯，我听见他的酣声，

深沉且温柔，
告诉我：不必在意人生的短促。

Mountain Crag
   by Meifu Wang

I journey away from home,
scattered thoughts scurrying behind like a little clerk.
Roving until dusk, I need not raise my head
to see the close of heaven's curtain.

He, more sudden than the night.
He, towering up in the deep blue sea.
He, using huge talons to stay the earth,

lives in the ice-cold sea, lives in the green-black sea.
His jagged shoulders bear the weight of destiny.
He goes with the earth's spin,
and turns his face to the wind and rain.

Consider how quietly my thoughts come, how quietly they
        go,
my days, likewise, waft to and fro.
Heaven sleeps in the bosom of the sea,
I hear his drunken snoring,

dark, now, and deep,
gentle, now, and soft,
telling me:
Must I live thinking life is too brief?

战俘

　　文 / 王美富

弹眼里若有一丝
残余的痉挛,
再补他一枪;
黑铁炼成的枪管
毫不迟疑。

啊,杏仁树,
我突然出奇地,
加倍爱你
黑色的铁钩。

刽子手的回答
抵制我问题的用意;
我设想他的语气
(还有那群旁观者的眼神)
会有一丝迟疑。

啊,杏仁树,
我着急地追忆
你的铁钩上绽放的花朵,
那一点儿心疼。

Prisoners of War
    by Meifu Wang

If there is still a convulsion,
or other sign of life in the bullet hole,
follow up with another shot.
The barrel of the rifle,
black tempered steel,
knows no hesitation.

Oh, almond tree,
suddenly I miss you,
doubly I love you,
your black iron hooks.

The executioner's answer
missed the center point;
I assumed his voice
might show a little hesitation.
I have not guessed the expressions
of the crowd of onlookers.

Oh, almond tree,
I recall your iron hooks
that puff out clouds of blossoms,
and a touch of red at the core,
sore-hearted looking.

狱墙外
两只野狗串在一起；
他们流浪的家族
并不寻思
太阳升起后的复仇。

啊，杏仁树，
你那么恣意，
雪白的花儿怒放，
无论在哪个异乡异地。

Outside the prison wall,
two dogs are coupling;
they are from the roaming clans,
and do not seek
revenge after the next sunrise.

Oh, almond tree,
you are so reckless,
snow white blossoms
in whatever foreign land
where you put down your roots.

致梅尔维尔

文 / 王美富

时间像蹉跎的马车
拖曳着走
我开始对夕阳失去耐心
它挥手告别 却慢条斯理
顺便把耀眼的金光撒满水面
彩霞也毫不迟疑地跨进窗户

但是我在等你
知道你和夜晚一起来

你不属于街上的那一伙
他们爱恋白日
依赖白日照亮身上的金色银色
朵朵娇艳的花
常有青头的蜜蜂飞来围舞
在艳阳下一起谈恋爱

但是我在等你
等你来了 那就像
北极光飞旋在太阳沉睡以后的天空
你魁梧的身材 是黑夜的魅影

啊 夜深如海
我对你的爱也深如大海。

To Melville
    by Meifu Wang

Time is dragging on like a horse-drawn cart.
I am losing patience watching the setting sun;
it waved farewell but malingers,
sprinkling golden speckles on the water,
flooding my room with rosy hues.

But I am waiting for you,
knowing you will come, blending in with the night.

You are not a member of the scene
that adores a sunny day, looking to the sun
to show off your gold and silver.
You are not in the company of brash flowers
to flirt with young honey bees,
in constant talk of love.

But I am waiting for you,
knowing you will come, blending in with the night.

A night forgotten by the sinking sun,
just right for the northern lights to cruise on by.
You will be here, mighty shadow.
You will be here, in the charming shade of night.

Oh night, deep as the sea,
I answer your love, deep as the sea.

Information about Contributors

The Editor-and-Translator Team 编译组:

王美富，出生于台湾，现任《廿一世纪中国诗歌》的主编兼翻译。曾获台湾大学外文学士，加州大学气象学硕士，普渡大学交通工程硕士。曾任世界银行交通专家，美国交通部工程师，阿拉斯加交通厅规划专家。现定居于华盛顿市，全心投入文学。

Meifu Wang: Ms. Wang is the chief editor and co-translator of *21st Century Chinese Poetry*. She was born and grew up in Taiwan, and earned her BA in Foreign Languages and Literature from National Taiwan University. She also received postgraduate degrees in physical and applied sciences, and worked in these fields for many years. Her poetry has appeared in various Chinese poetry journals. She lives in Washington DC.

苏浪禹，出生于华盛顿市，现任《廿一世纪中国诗歌》的翻译。曾做过潜水艇水手，报社编辑人员，政府行政主管。在报社工作期间，基于对字体的研究，加上业余时间集邮的嗜好，使他对中国文字产生浓厚的兴趣，并尝试翻译汉语诗歌。他的著作包括四本个人诗集。苏先生从华盛顿退休以后与妻子居住于北卡罗来纳州。

Michael Truman Soper: Mr. is the co-translator of *21st Century Chinese Poetry*. Born in Washington, DC, in 1946, he began writing poetry in high school, and studied creative writing, briefly, at UVA. He was a submarine sailor during the Vietnam War, after that, a newspaper typesetter and night school student. His degree is in Business Administration. His career led from printing and publishing to contract management. Fascinated by Chinese character fonts, he began translating Chinese poetry almost 20 years ago. He is retired, living in North Carolina with his wife, Mary Lou. He has published four e-books of poetry.

唐晓飞，出生于美国德州，幼年时在欧洲长大。唐晓飞先生担任《廿一世纪中国诗歌》的修改和校对。唐先生任职于史密森尼博物馆，曾翻译意大利文，西班牙文，和法文诗歌。他住在华盛顿市。

Steven Townsend: Mr. Townsend participated in the review and revision of *21st Century Chinese Poetry*. Born in the US but spent considerable time in Europe as a child, Mr. Townsend writes poetry as well as translates poetry from French, Spanish, and Italian to English. He has published some of his poetic works as Kindle e-books. Mr. Townsend lives in Washington DC.

张凡修，1958年生，河北玉田人，中国作协会员。1975年高中毕业后在家乡玉田县务农。诗歌刊发于《诗刊》等诸多刊物，著有诗集《地气》等三部。2010年，被《诗刊》社、《星星》诗刊社联合评为中国十大农民诗人。自第七辑开始，张凡修先生参与《廿一世纪中国诗歌》的选稿工作。

Zhang Fanxiu: Starting from 2013, Mr. Zhang Fanxiu participated in the selection of poems for *21st Century Chinese Poetry*. He was born in 1958 in Hebei Province, and has been a farmer since graduating from high school in 1975. He moved to the remote western region of Liaoning Province in 2007, and has since produced hundreds of poems that reveal his unique insight into nature, the land and rural life. His work can be seen in various major literary journals in China. He has also published three collections of poems: *Writings from the Moors*, *The Spirit of the Earth*, and *Only the Earth*.

Poets (listed in alphabetical order):

陈敏：西北大学中文系毕业，安康市《旅途》杂志编辑。出版了个人作品集及主编系列作品《蓝星星》《金月亮》《这方天空》《我们》和《安康作家优秀作品选》。
Chen Min: Chen Min graduated from Chinese Department of Northwest University, Xi'an, Shan'xi, He works as the editor of *The Journey*, a popular magazine in the City of Ankang, Shan'xi
Province.

黄礼孩，生于大陆最南端的徐闻县，现居广州。戏剧创作专业毕业曾在中山大学、北京大学读书。诗歌在《诗刊》、《星星》、《诗歌月刊》、《诗选刊》、《上海文学》、《青年文学》、《大家》等刊发表。出版诗集《我对命运所知甚少》等多部。
Huang Lihai: Mr. Huang Lihai was born in Xuwen, the southernmost township of China, Mr. Huang studied Drama in Zhongshan University and Beijing University. He lives and works in Guangzhou of Guangdong Province. His poetry has appeared in various Chinese poetry journals. He has also published several poetry collections, including *The Little I Know about Destiny*.

李云，女，笔名七月的海，山东人。出版诗集《七月的海》《七月的海诗选》《最美的神》《李云短诗选》(双语版)。诗观：诗歌，让我无限地接近世界、又无限地接近自我，所以我写着、爱着......

Li Yun (pen name: The Sea of July): Ms. Li works and lives in Shandong Province. She approaches poetry with the following philosophy: "To write is to love. Through poetry, I become infinitely close to the world, and infinitely close to myself." She has published several books of poetry, among them *The Sea of July* and *Short Poems by Li Yun*.

娜夜，满族。祖籍辽宁兴城，成长于西北。毕业于南京大学中文系，二十世纪八十年代中期开始诗歌写作，曾获鲁迅文学奖。现居兰州，供职某报社。诗歌集：《回味爱情》、《冰唇》、《娜夜诗选》、《娜夜的诗》

Na Ye: Ms. Na Ye was born in Liaoning Province of Manchurian descent, but grew up in China's northwest region. She graduated from the Chinese Department of Nanjing University. She has published four poetry collections, among them *Savoring Love*, *Cold Lips*, and *Poems by Na Ye*, and received the prestigious Luxun Literary Award for her poetic works. She lives and works in Gansu Province as a journalist.

宋惠元，笔名柳思，浙江湖州人，杭州大学毕业。出版四本诗集，《红枕》和《渡》等。他说：我不为诗歌而活着，我是因为活着（或者说为了活得更好）才写诗歌。现任职杭州日报。

Song Huiyuan(penname: Liusi): Mr. Song graduated from Hangzhou University. His lyrical poems are widely admired and can be found in many poetry journals in China. He has published four poetry collections. Mr. Song works for Hangzhou Daily News and presently lives in Hangzhou.

宋雨,北疆人。祖籍青海。2008年开始习诗,作品见于《汉诗》、《金台诗刊》、《新世纪诗典》、《诗刊》、《诗歌月刊》、《被一代:中国诗歌十年档案》等刊。出版自撰诗集《我听我说》。

Song Yu: Ms. Song Yu was born and now lives in Xinjiang Autonomous Prefecture, China. She began writing poetry in 2008, and her works can now be seen in various literary journals in China. She has published one poetry collection: *I Listen to Myself*.

王美富,出生于台湾,现任《廿一世纪中国诗歌》的主编兼翻译。曾获台湾大学外文学士,加州大学气象学硕士,普渡大学交通工程硕士。曾任世界银行交通专家,美国交通部工程师,阿拉斯加交通厅规划专家。现定居于华盛顿市,全心投入文学。

Meifu Wang: Ms. Wang is the chief editor and co-translator of 21st Century Chinese Poetry. She was born and grew up in Taiwan, and earned her BA in Foreign Languages and Literature from National Taiwan University. She also received postgraduate degrees in physical and applied sciences, and worked in these fields for many years. Her poetry has appeared in various Chinese poetry journals. She lives in Washington DC.

巫丁，汉语名苏华，回族。族名纳素巫丁,祖籍新疆和田，生于四川宜宾。1980年代习诗，1982年在花城出版社《青年诗坛》创刊号上发表组诗(自己之歌)九首。继后在《诗刊》、《星星诗刊》、《诗歌报月刊》、《十月》《青年作家》等杂志发有作品。曾任职多家图书公司，编辑出版过多种图书。现居重庆。
Wuding: Mr. Wuding was born in Sichuan Province of Hui descent, China. Mr. Wuding studied French in the University, and worked for various publishing houses afterwards. His poetry has appeared in various Chinese poetry journals. He now lives in Chongqing.

姚风，原名姚京明，诗人，翻译家。生于北京，后移居澳门，现任教于澳门大学葡文系。著有中葡文诗集《写在风的翅膀上》、《一条地平线，两种风景》、《瞬间的旅行》、《黑夜与我一起躺下》、《远方之歌》、《当鱼闭上眼睛》以及译著《葡萄牙现代诗选》、《澳门中葡诗歌选》、《安德拉德诗选》、《中国当代十诗人作品选》等十多部。
Yao Feng（Penname of Yao Jingming）: Mr. Yao was born in Beijing in 1958. He received his doctorate degree in comparative literature from Fudan University in Shanghai, and currently works as an associate professor in the Department of Portuguese at the University of Macau. In addition to translating Portuguese poets into Chinese, he has also published several poetry collections, both in Chinese and in Portuguese, among them *On the Wings of the Wind*, *The Night Lies Down with Me*, and *Song of Faraway Places*. He is the recipient of several literary awards.

翟文熙，一九七三年生，诗歌作品零散发表于各种刊物及选集。

Zhai Wenxi: Born in 1973, Mr. Zhai writes poetry, prose and essays, but has turned more to poetry since the late 1990s. His writings have been published in various Chinese literary journals. Mr. Zhai lives in Guangzhou.

Cover Page Artist:

<杏仁花开> (印章), 艺术家：**十画**, (肖维振)， 宁夏，银川

<Almond Blossom> Chinese Seal Carving, by Xiao Weizhen, a young artist specialized in traditional Chinese arts. He lives in Ningxia Province, China.

Contact Information:

You are welcome to write to the editors of *21ˢᵗ Century Chinese Poetry* at the following address, and we will try our best to answer your questions.

editor@modernchinesepoetry.com

We invite you to visit our web page:

www.ModernChinesePoetry.com

PAPB
3.99

8/27/2024

Made in the USA
Charleston, SC
06 July 2013